Start Reading
TOGETHER

Children Around the World

Verna Wilkins

QED Publishing

First published in the UK in 2004 by
QED Publishing
A Quarto Group Company
226 City Road
London, EC1V 2TT

www.qed-publishing.co.uk

A Catalogue record for this book is available from the British Library.

ISBN 1 84538 312 5

Written by Verna Wilkins
Designed by Zeta Jones
Editor Hannah Ray
Picture Researcher Joanne Beardwell

Series Consultant Anne Faundez
Creative Director Louise Morley
Editorial Manager Jean Coppendale

Printed and bound in China

Picture credits

Key: t = top, b = bottom, m = middle, c = centre, l = left, r = right

Corbis/Anthony Bannister 14tr, /Owen Franken 10tc, /So Hing-Keung 6–7,
/Wolfgang Kaehler 10–11, /David Katzenstein 12–13, /Earl & Nazima Kowall 13t, /Jacques
Langevin 20–21, /Lawrence Manning 17t, /Stephanie Maze 16–17, /Paul A Souders 14–15,
/Tom Stewart 21bl, /Staffan Widstrand 8–9; **Trip**/Helene Rogers 4–5, 18–19.

Contents

Britain

"I am Janet. My best friend is Kim. We both live in London, in England.

We walk together to our big, new school. We love playtime.

My favourite food is pizza.

My favourite game is football."

America

"I am Amy. I live in New York. New York is full of tall buildings called skyscrapers.

I love baseball. My favourite team is the Yankees. I play Little League baseball every Saturday.

My mum is a doctor. Dad is a teacher."

Canada

"My name is Kipanik. I live near Iqaluit, in northern Canada.

I go to school in a **snowmobile**. When my dad was little, he rode a dog sledge.

I love stories about long ago.

I like making snowmen as big as me!"

Brazil

"My name is Davi. My home is near a river in the rainforest. At night, I sleep in a **hammock** which hangs from the ceiling.

I swim in the river with my two older sisters and brother. They never leave me to swim alone. There are alligators in the river."

11

India

"I am Kamal. I can speak Hindi and English. Lila is my little sister.

My father drives me to school in his taxi. Writing stories is my favourite lesson at school."

Africa

"Jambo! That means 'hello' in Swahili, my language. I am Asha. I live in Kenya.

Dad takes visitors to see the lions, zebra, cheetahs and elephants that live near my home.

When I grow up, I want to write books about animals."

China

"I am Lin. I live in Beijing.

I like going to school
with my friends.

At home, I love watching
cartoons on TV.

My little sister is learning
to eat with chopsticks."

Australia

"I am named Alice, after Alice Springs. My mother was born there. My father was born in England. We live near Perth, in Western Australia.

I have just learned to swim and ride my bike. We often have **barbecues** in the garden.

I've seen lots of kangaroos and koalas. My favourite animal is the koala."

19

Caribbean

"I am Lola. My school is near the beach, in St Lucia. This is a hot country. Sometimes we have lessons outside.

I love to play **hopscotch** and to skip in the playground.

My dad is a fireman. My mum is a teacher. I have one older brother. His name is Levi.

My favourite food is rice and peas."

Glossary

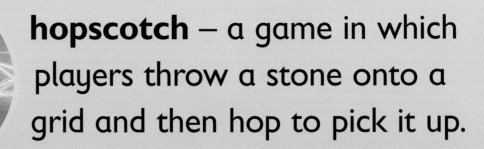

barbecue – a way of cooking food outdoors using burning charcoal.

hammock – a piece of cloth that is hung above the ground and used to lie or sleep in.

hopscotch – a game in which players throw a stone onto a grid and then hop to pick it up.

snowmobile – a special motor vehicle for travelling over snow.

Index

Carers' and teachers' notes

- Look at the front cover together, and ask your child to predict what the book is about. Read the title together.
- Explain that the book gives us information, rather than tells us a story, and that this type of book is known as non-fiction. Find the contents page, the glossary and the index. Tell your child that these features are often found in non-fiction books.
- Read about Amy (page 6), and then ask your child to talk about his/her own life. Does your child live in a high-rise building? Would he/she like to be a doctor, just like Amy's mum, when he/she grows up?
- Read about Janet (page 5), and then help your child to write a few sentences about himself/herself. Encourage your child to introduce himself/herself, to name his/her best friend, to say where he/she lives and to describe what he/she likes about school.
- Ask your child to draw a self-portrait. Attach it to his/her writing.

- Read about Asha (page 14). Use an atlas or a globe to find a map of Kenya.
- Draw pictures of a lion, a zebra, a cheetah and an elephant.
- Read about Alice (page 18). Find out, using a map, where Alice Springs is.
- Use reference books to find information about koala bears and kangaroos.
- Look at the picture of Kipanik going to school in a snowmobile (page 9). Ask your child to explain how he/she gets to school.
- What other ways are there of going to school? Read through the texts and look at the pictures to find out. (Kamal, on page 13, goes to school in a taxi called an auto-rickshaw.)
- Talk about similarities. What are some of the things that children all over the world like to do? For example, watch cartoons on TV, play with their friends, listen to stories, play hopscotch, play sports.